Artists see the flaws in their own work. This is part of the driving force of creativity — seeking to share what you see in yourself & the world around you. The beauty mingles with the hideous, the mistake with the sublime. An artists eye is always striving to share the truest expression of their surroundings; the reality of their existence. But that eye doesn't know how others interpretations will be formed. This is the unspoken relationship between artist and observer.

Collected here is one of the most raw, thoughtfully depicted collections of multi-faceted concepts, complex ideas, and deep emotions I have seen put to paper. The shared struggle of human existence is examined & illustrated organically, dripping with humorous insight.

I am proud & excited to witness the evolution of Cody reflected in his art.

Cody, as you refine your craft you illuminate the truth of your surroundings.

Truth is always worth saving.

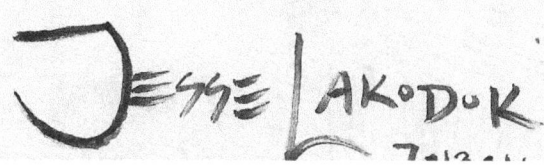
Jesse Lakoduk

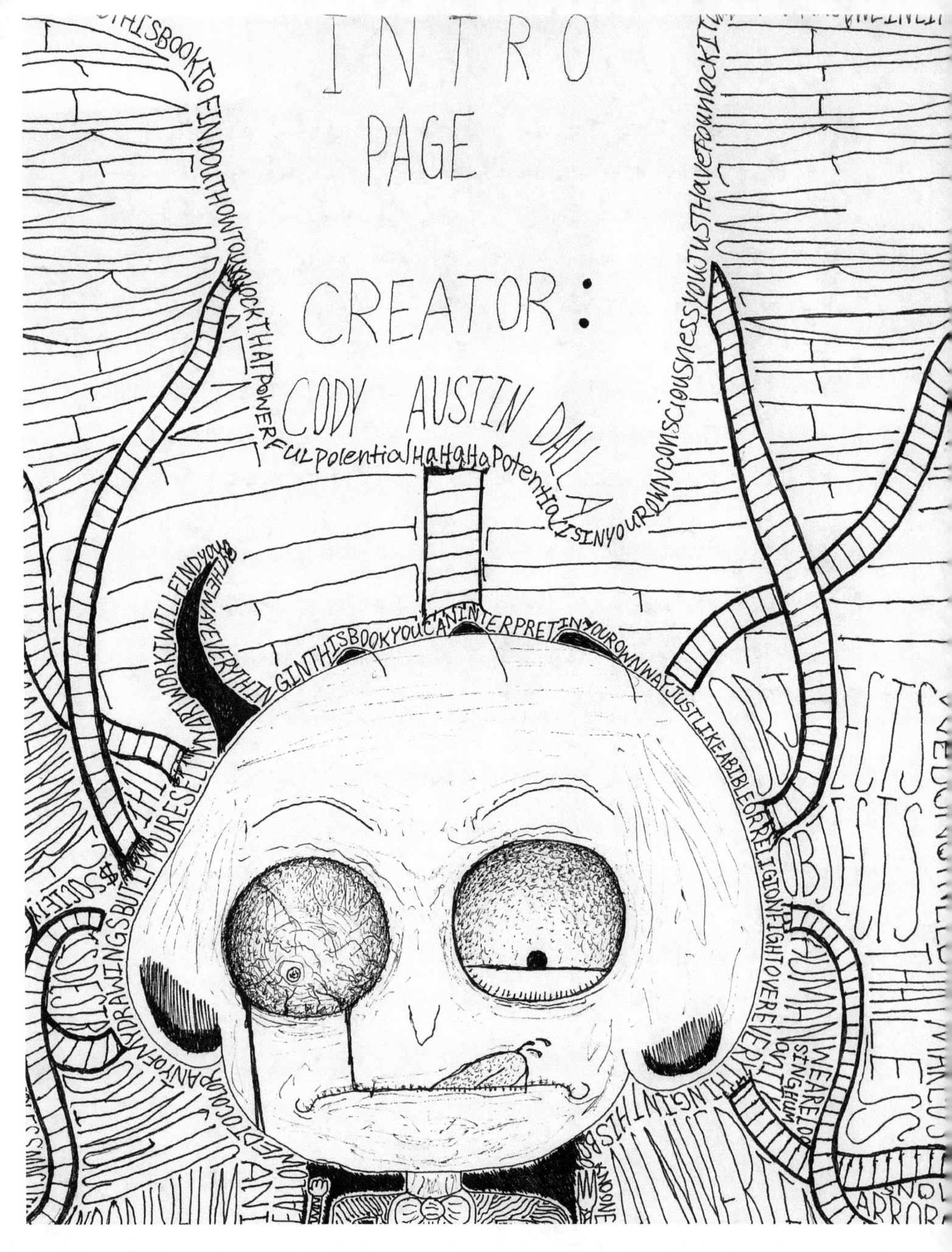

INTRO
PAGE

CREATOR:

CODY AUSTIN DALLA

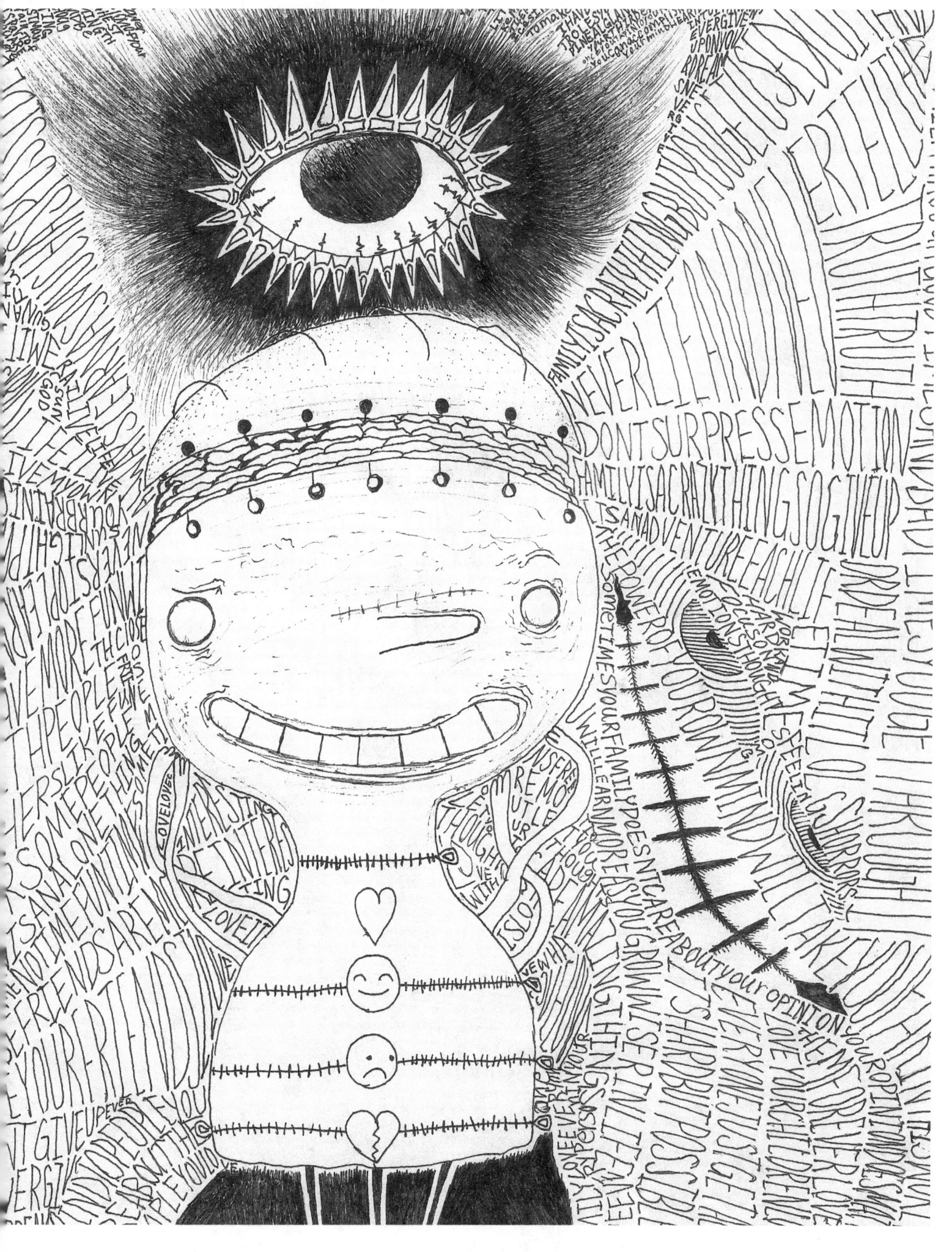

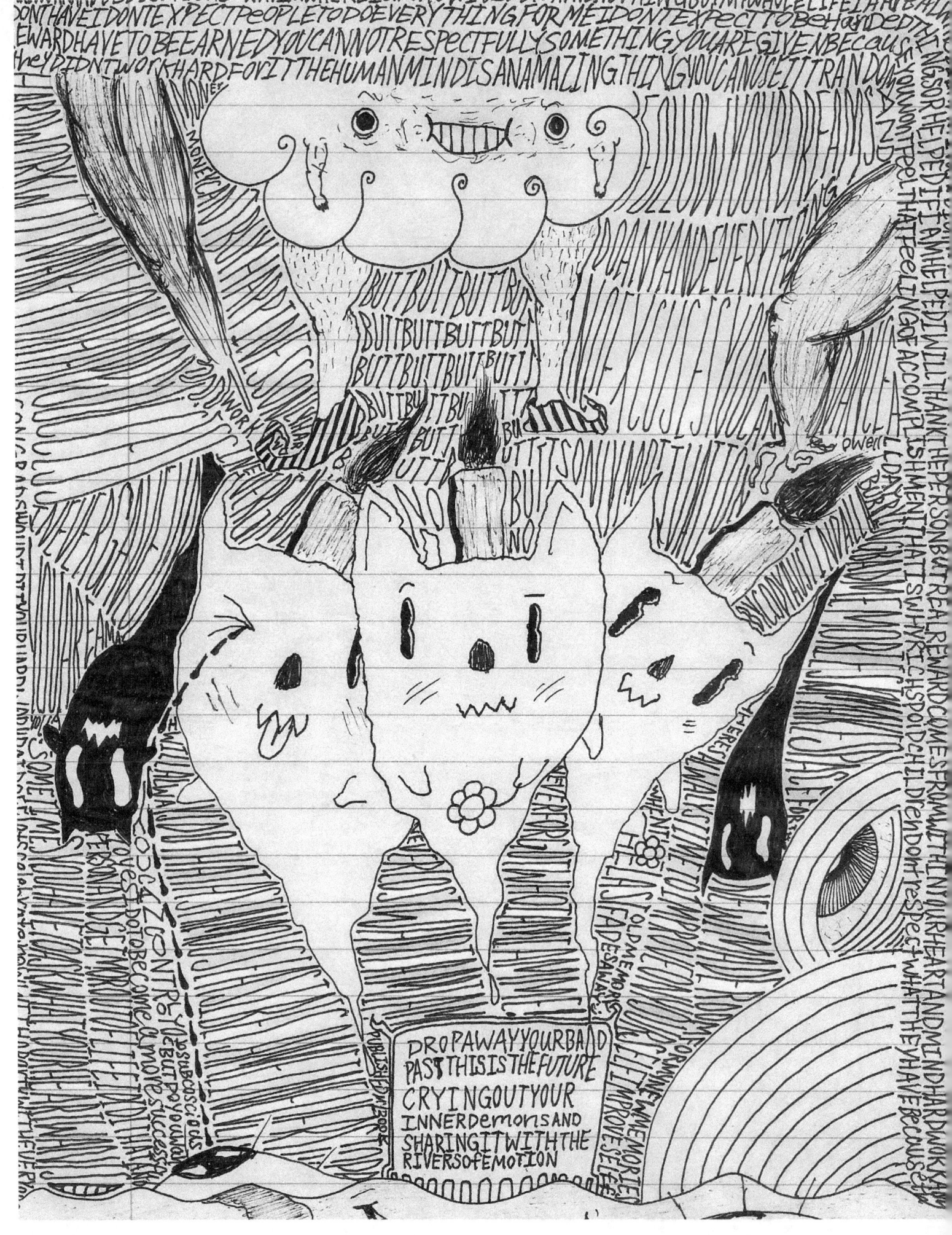

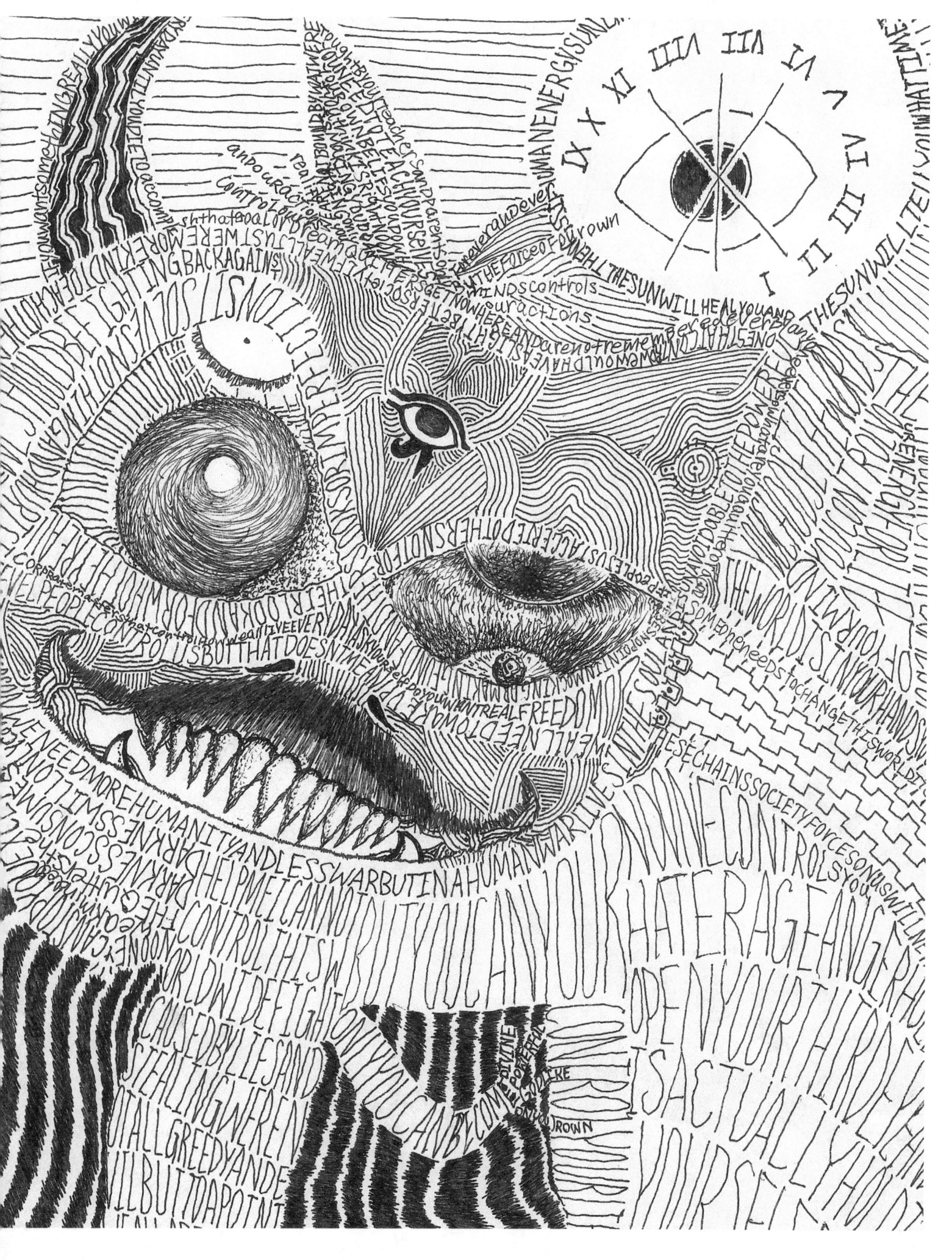

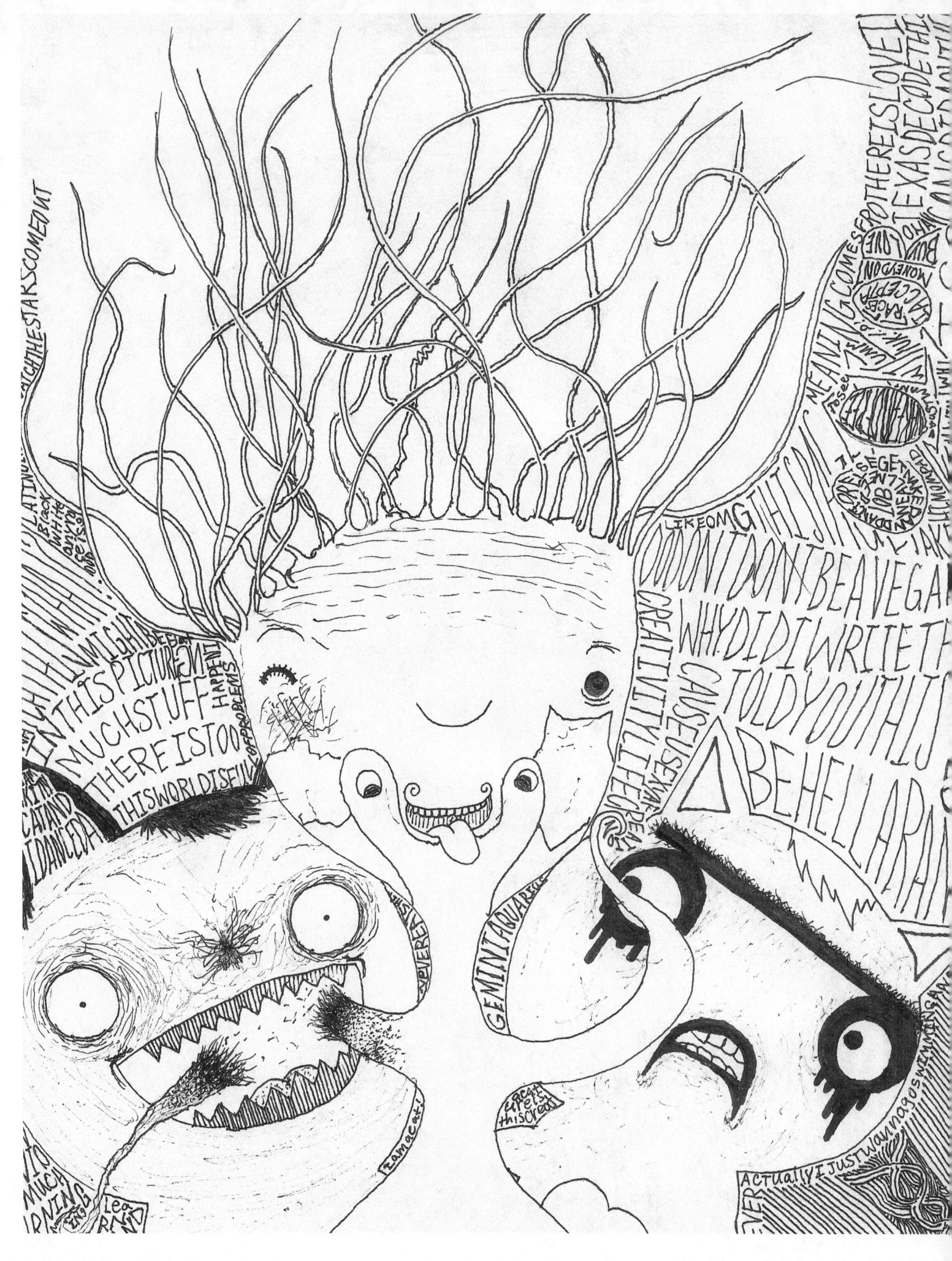

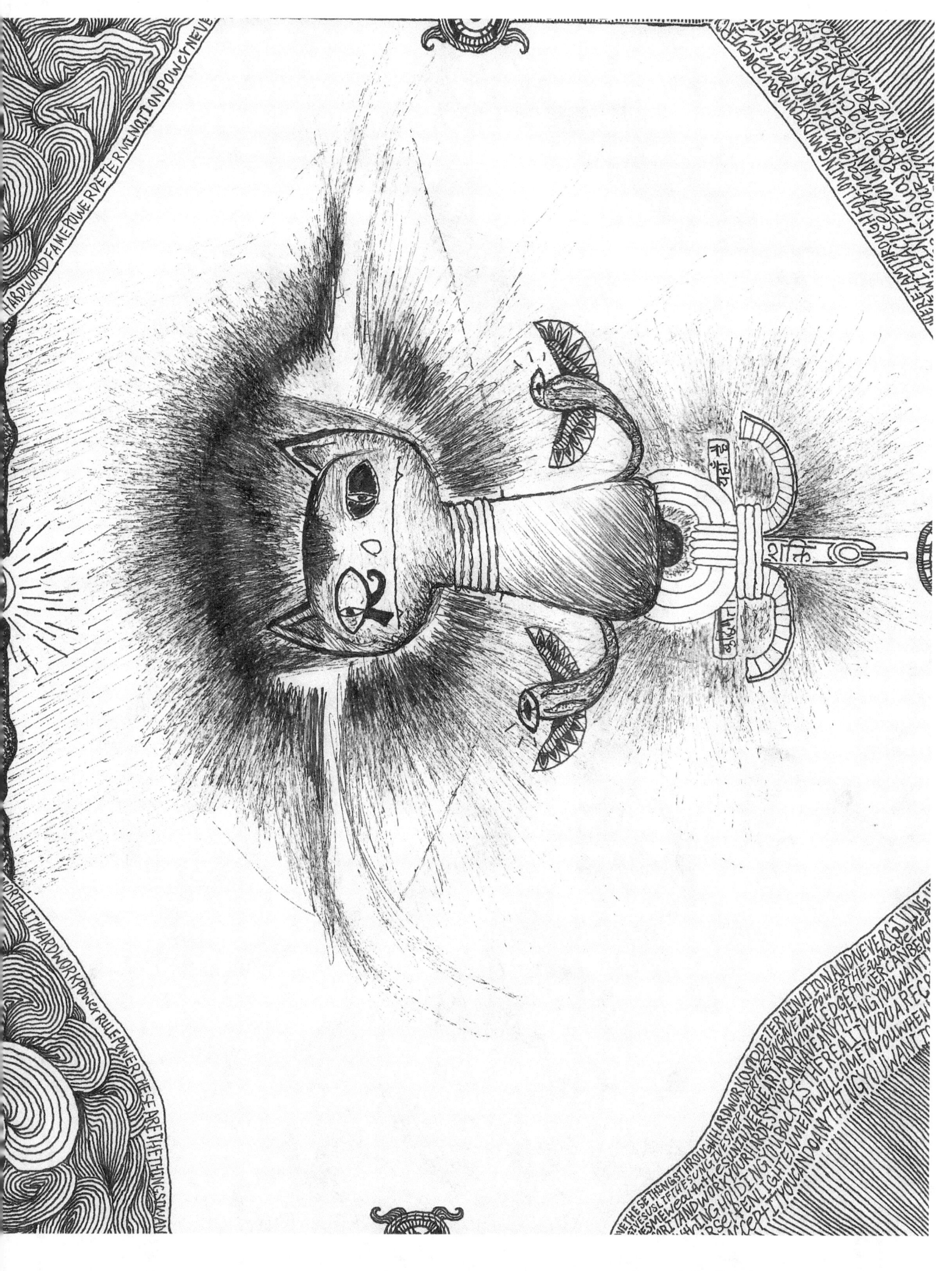

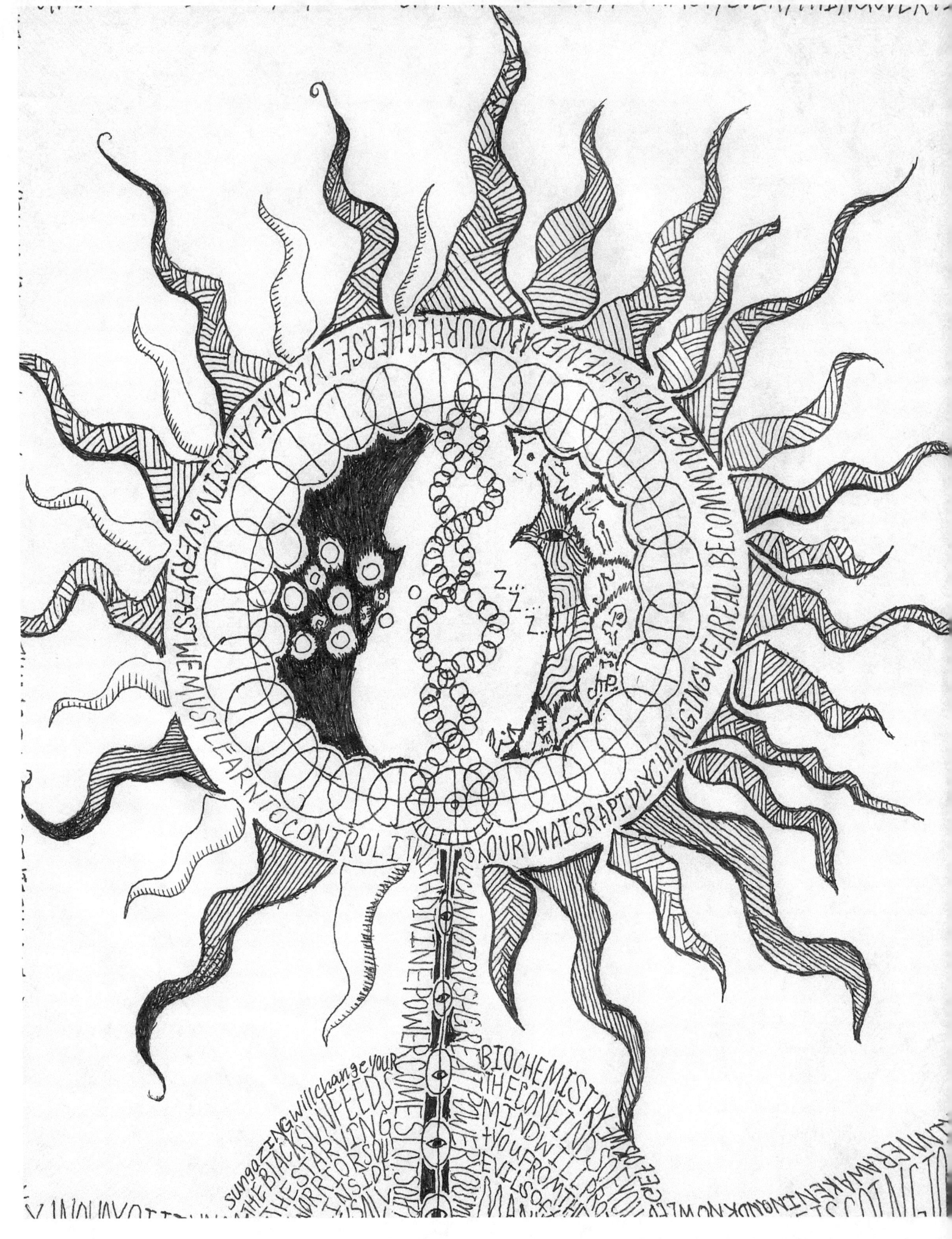

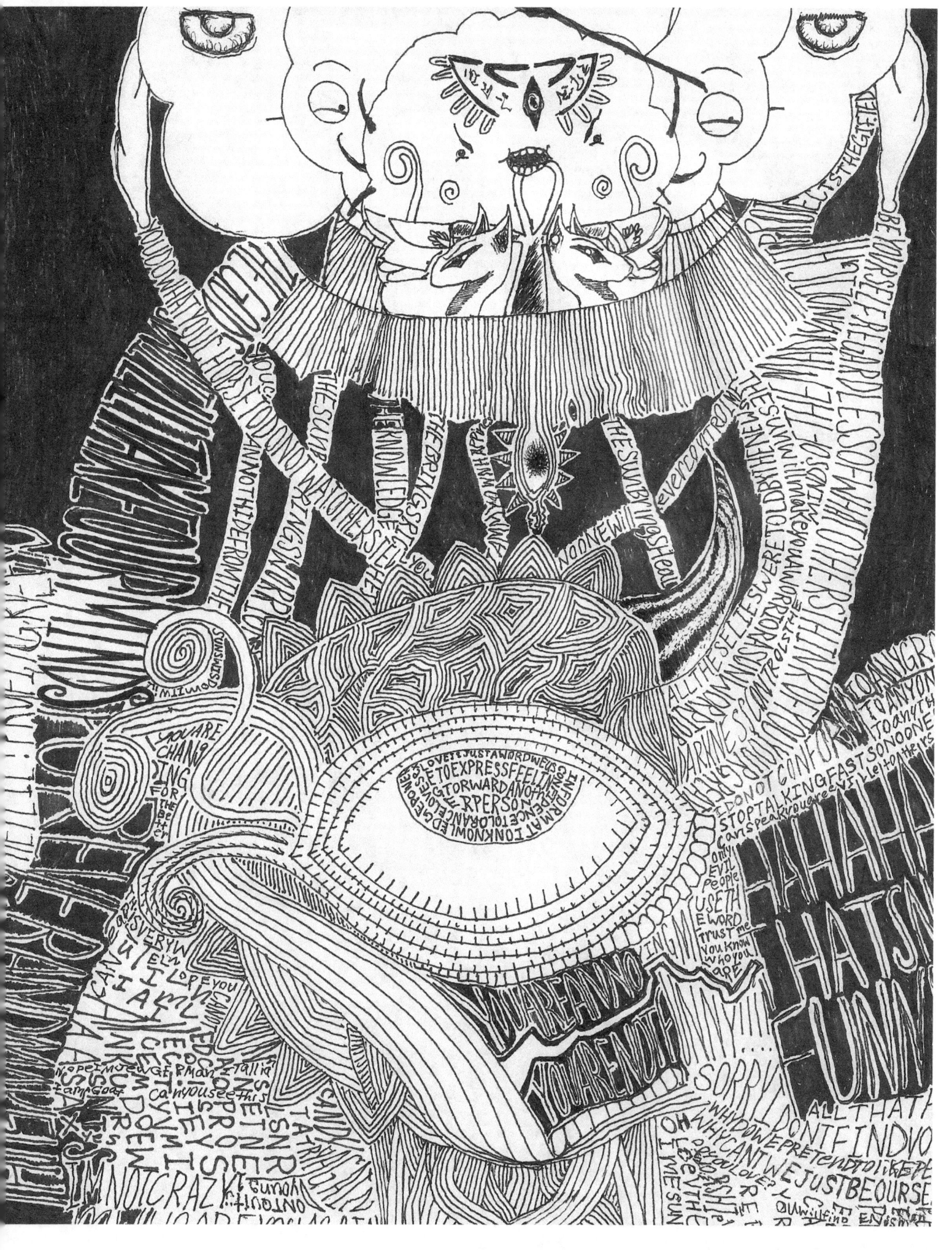

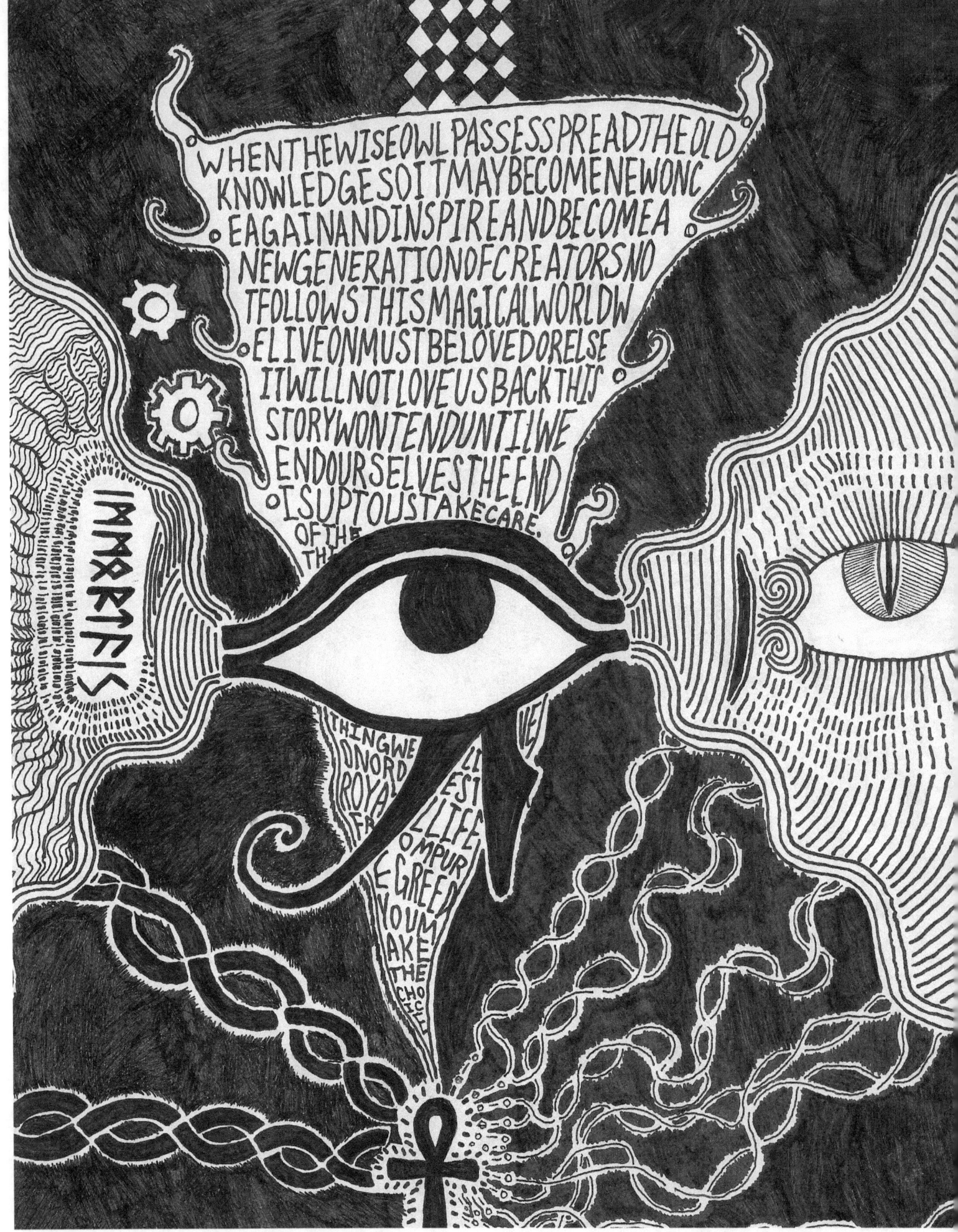

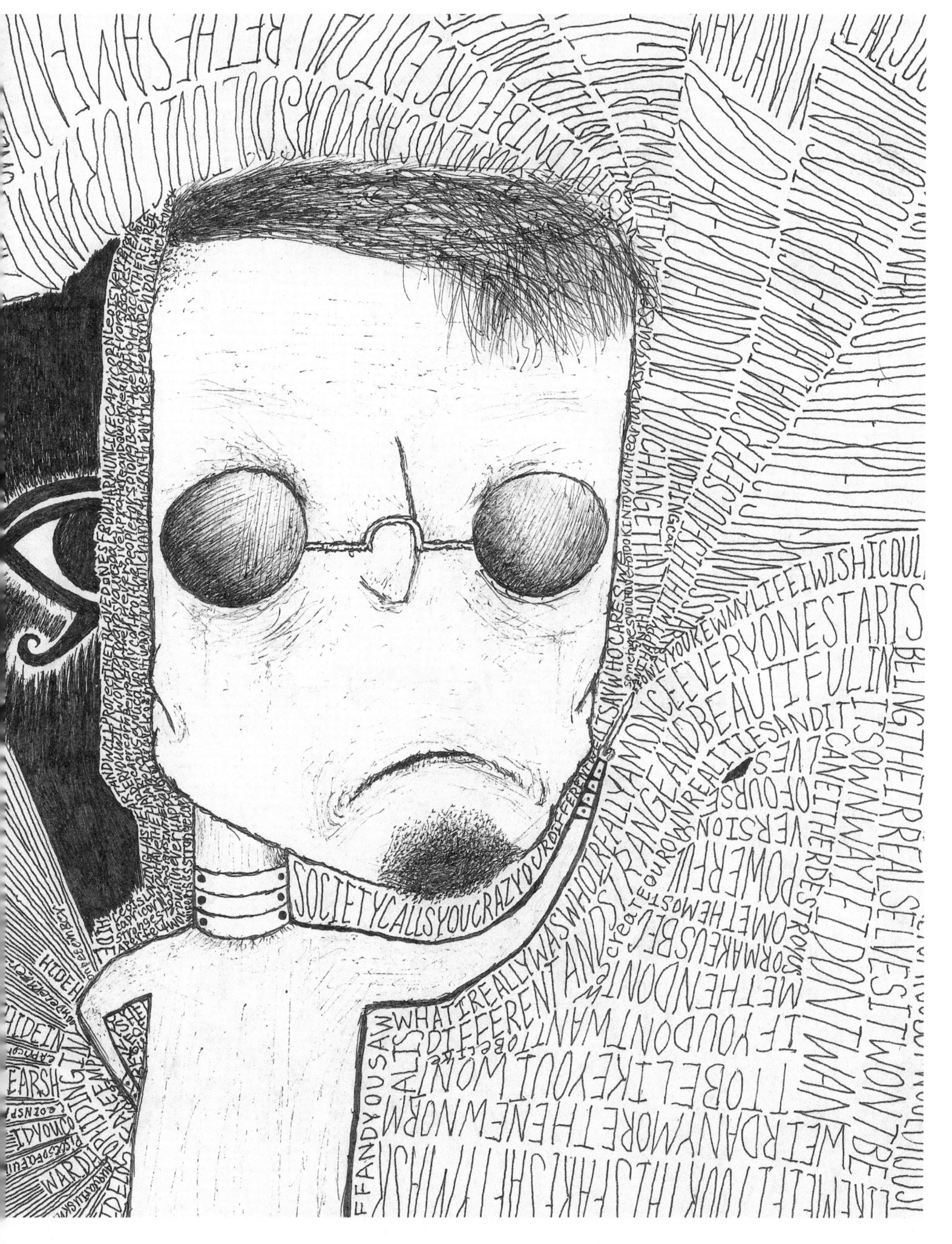

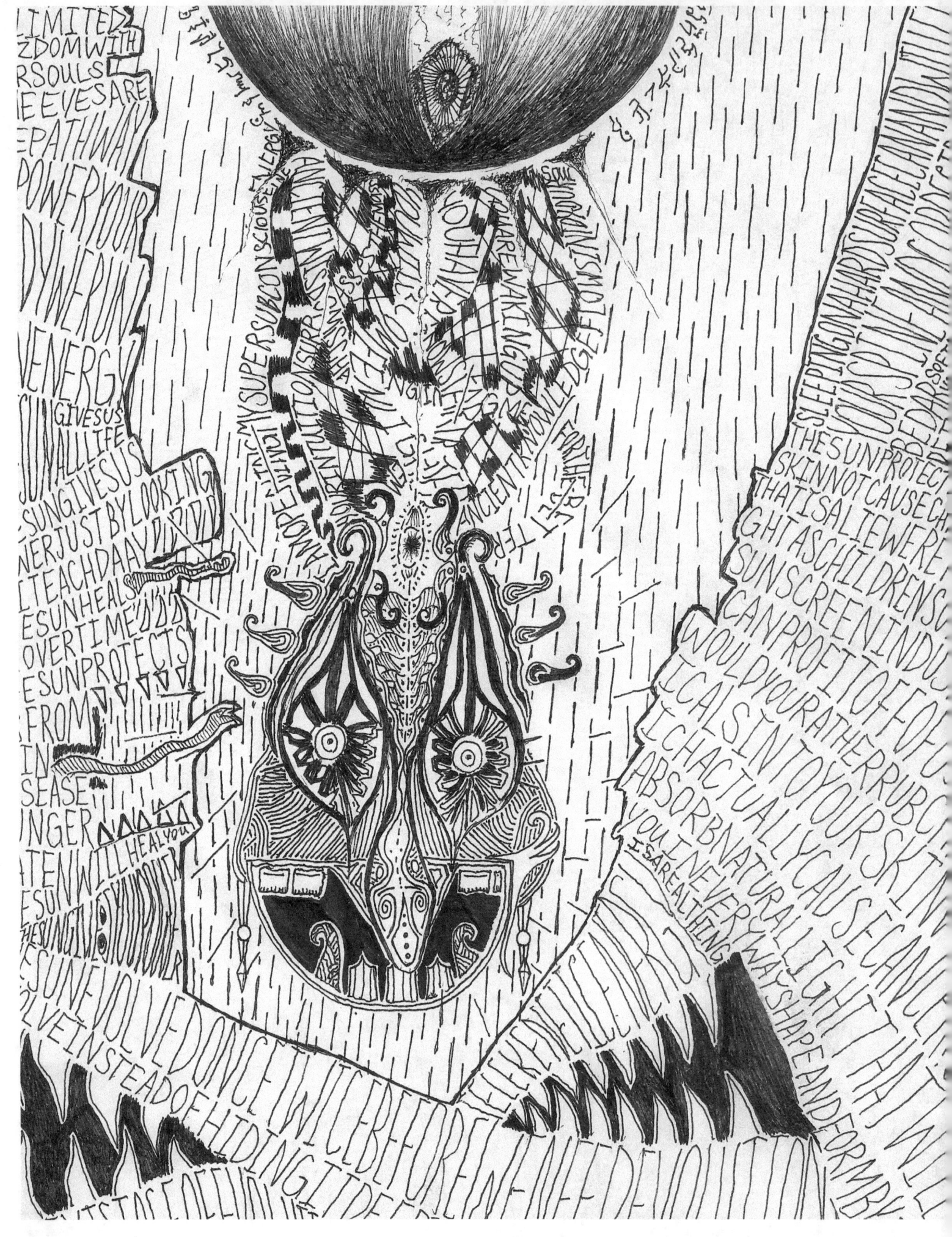

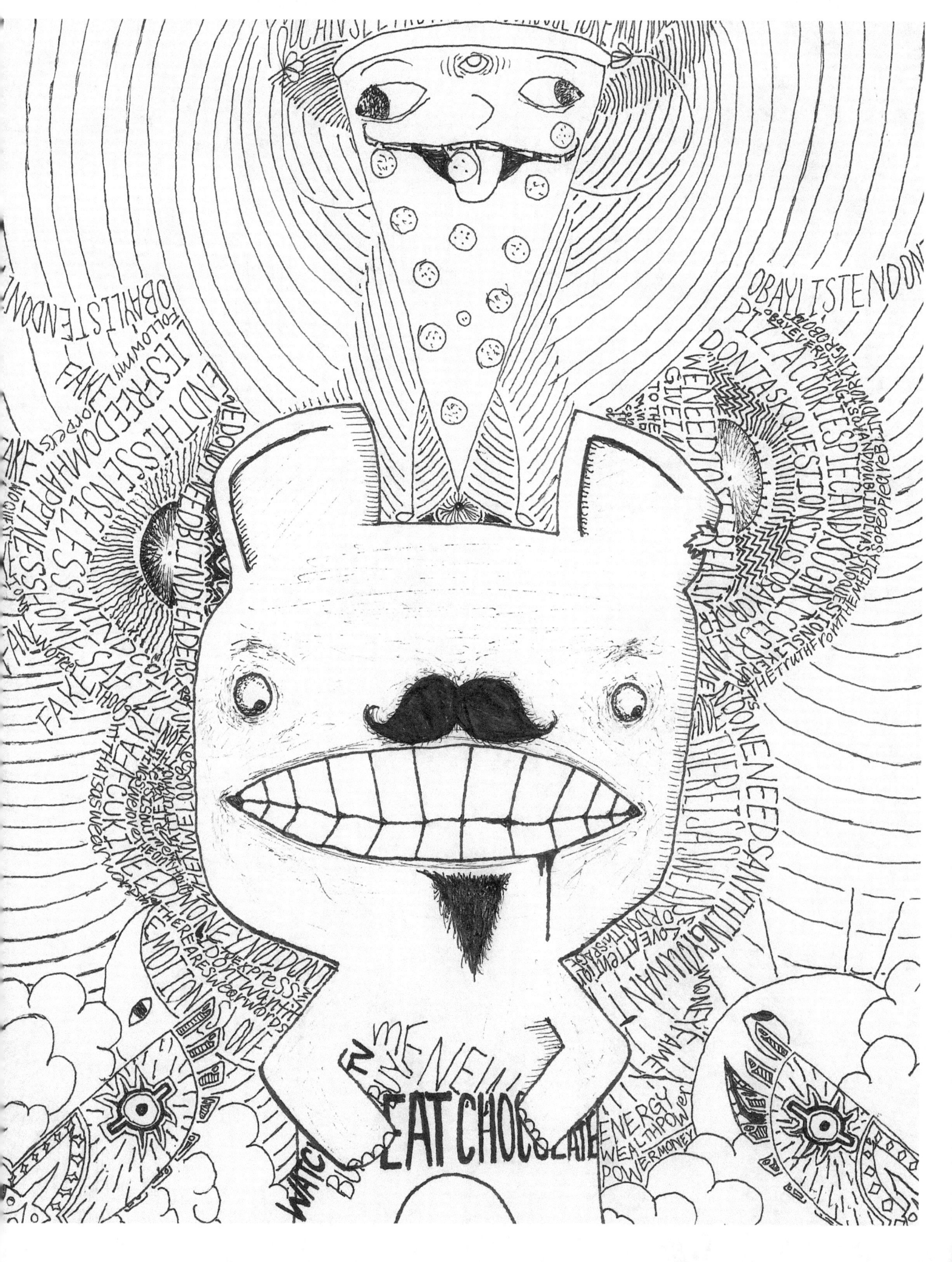

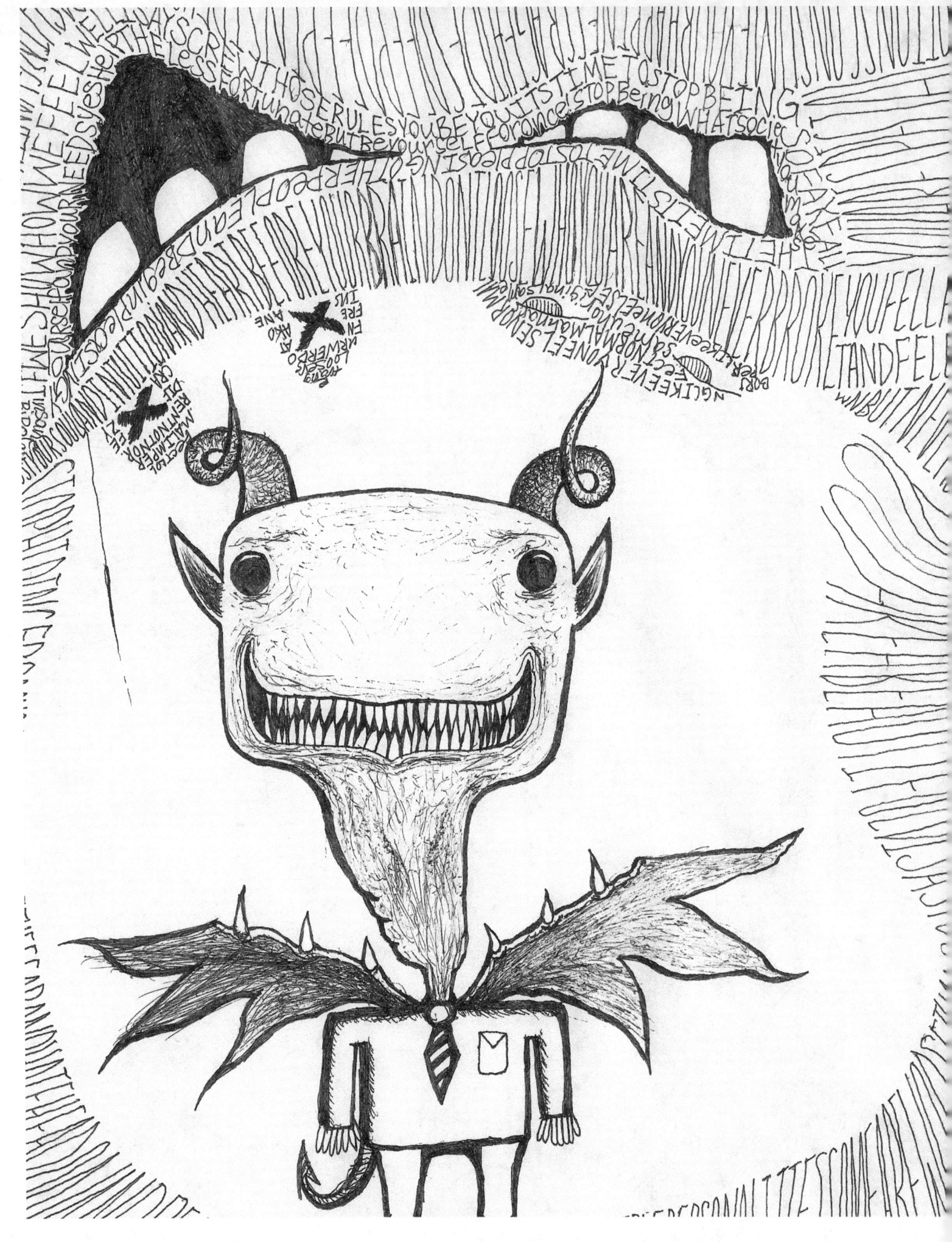

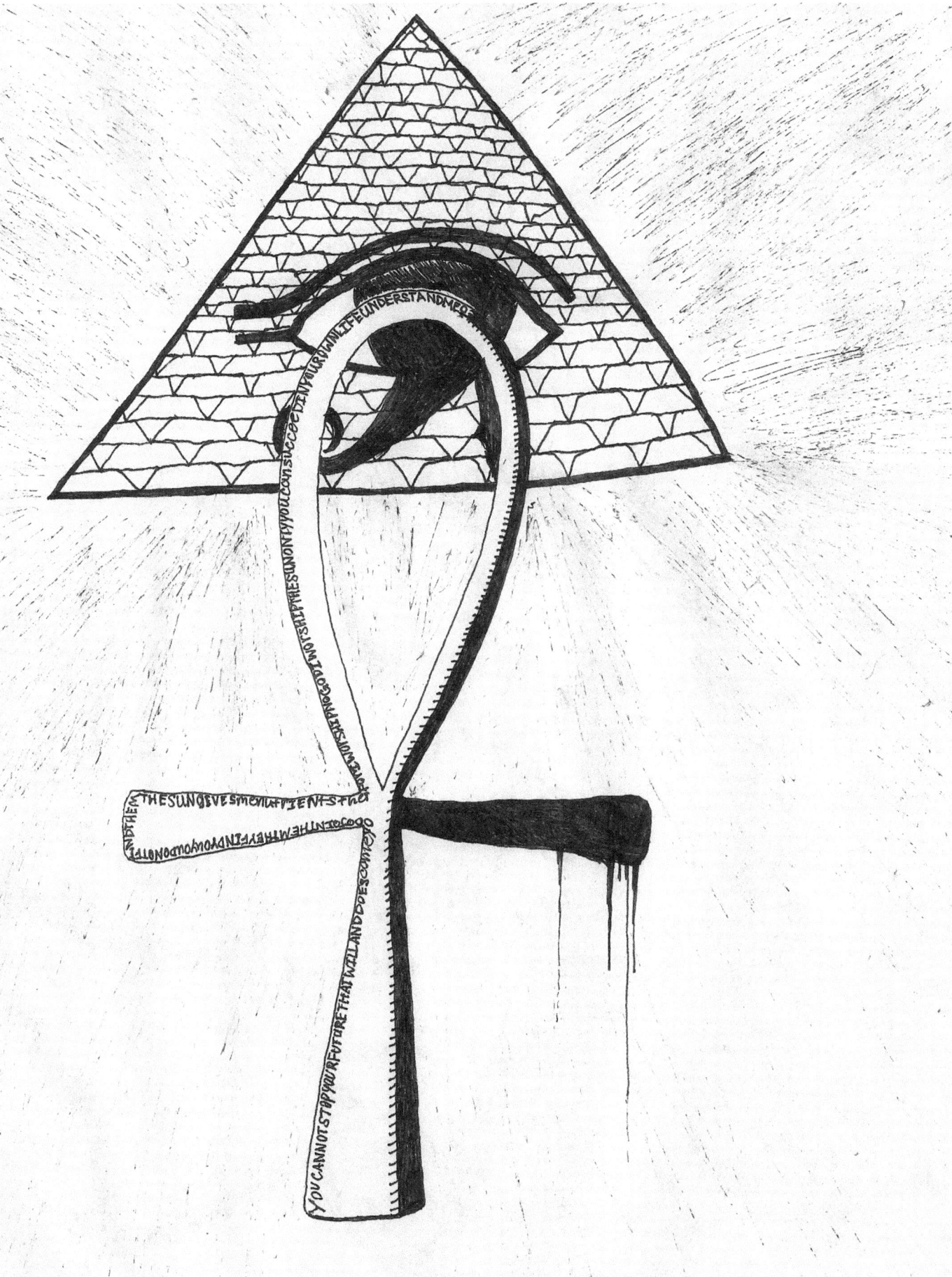

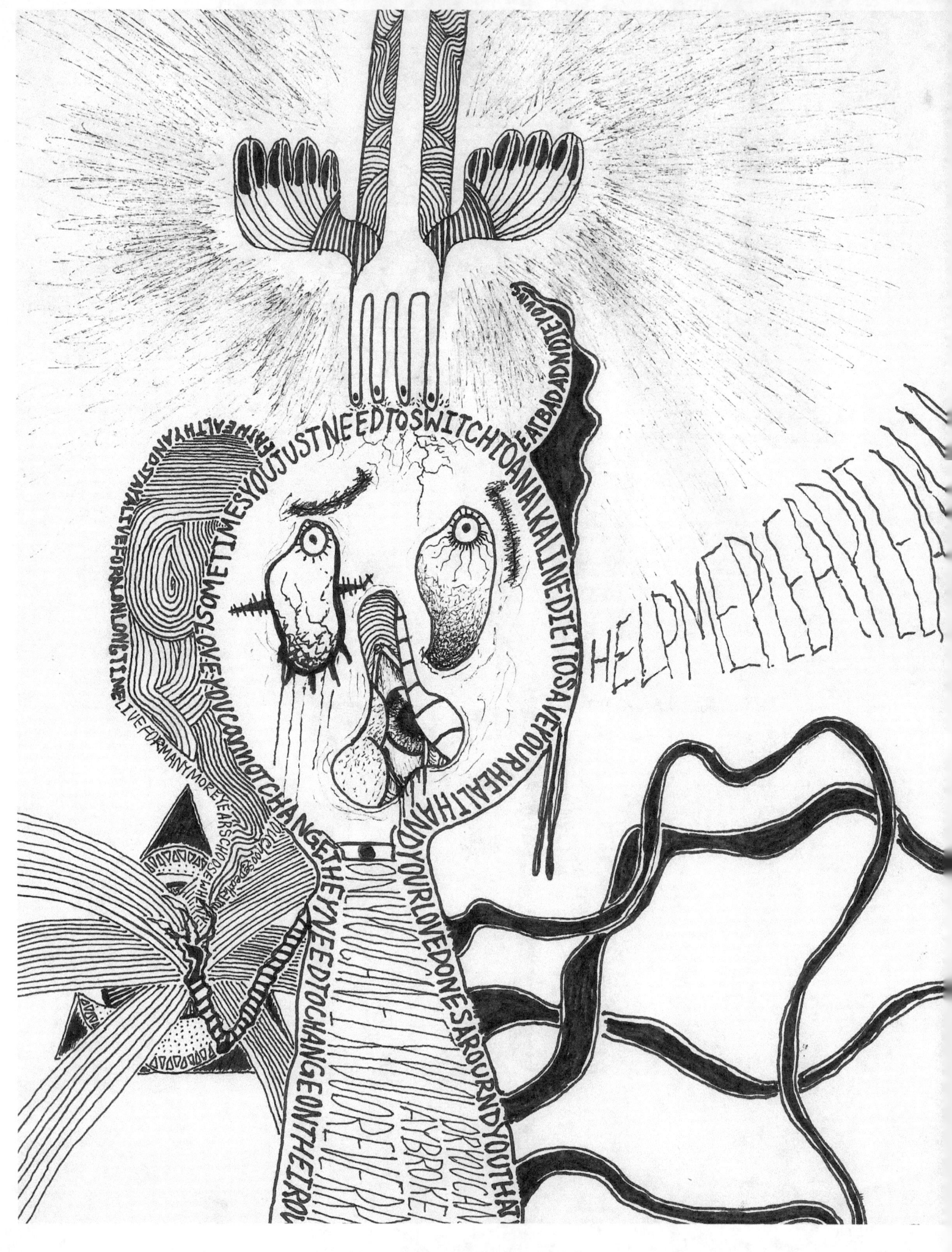

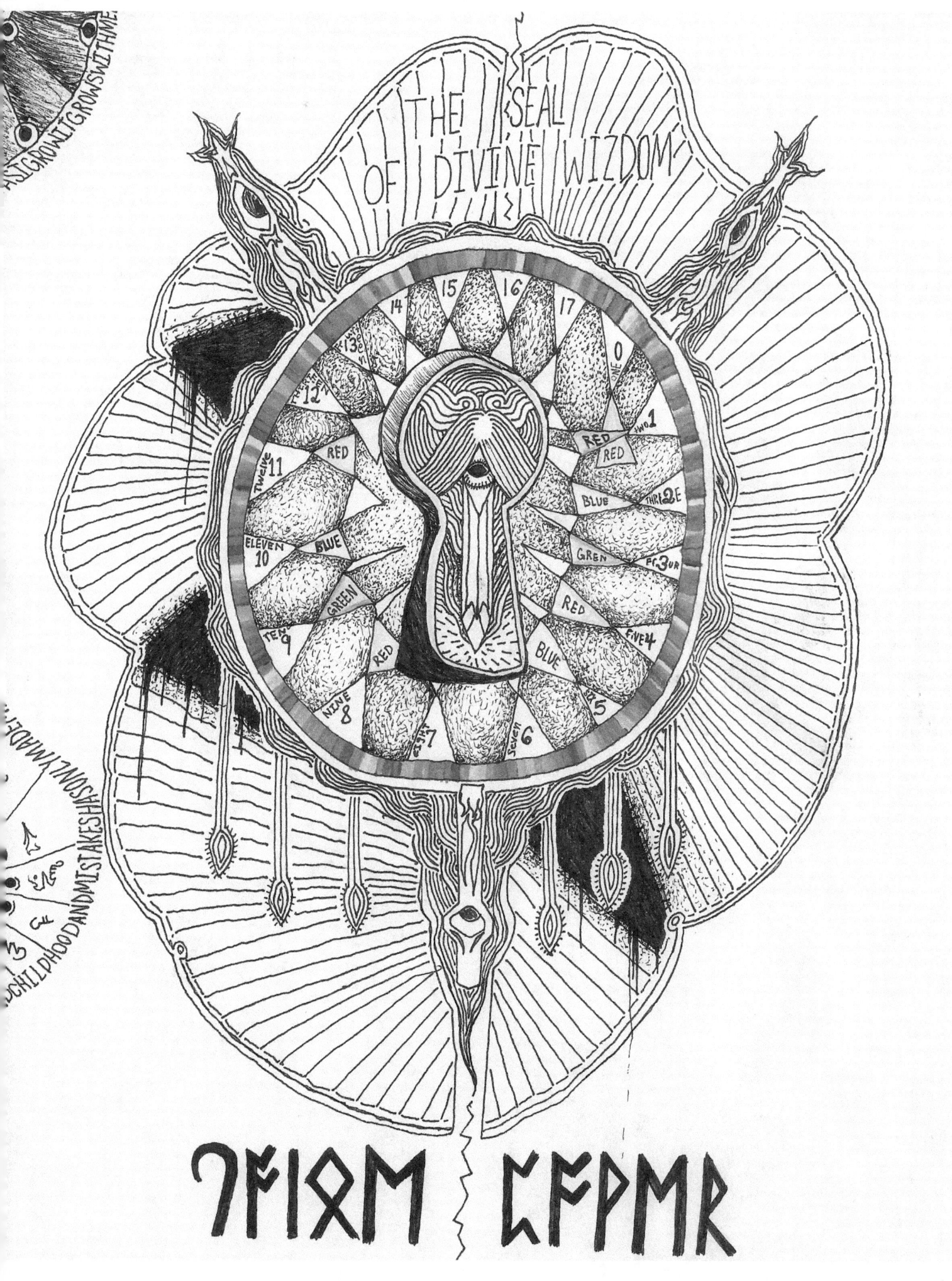

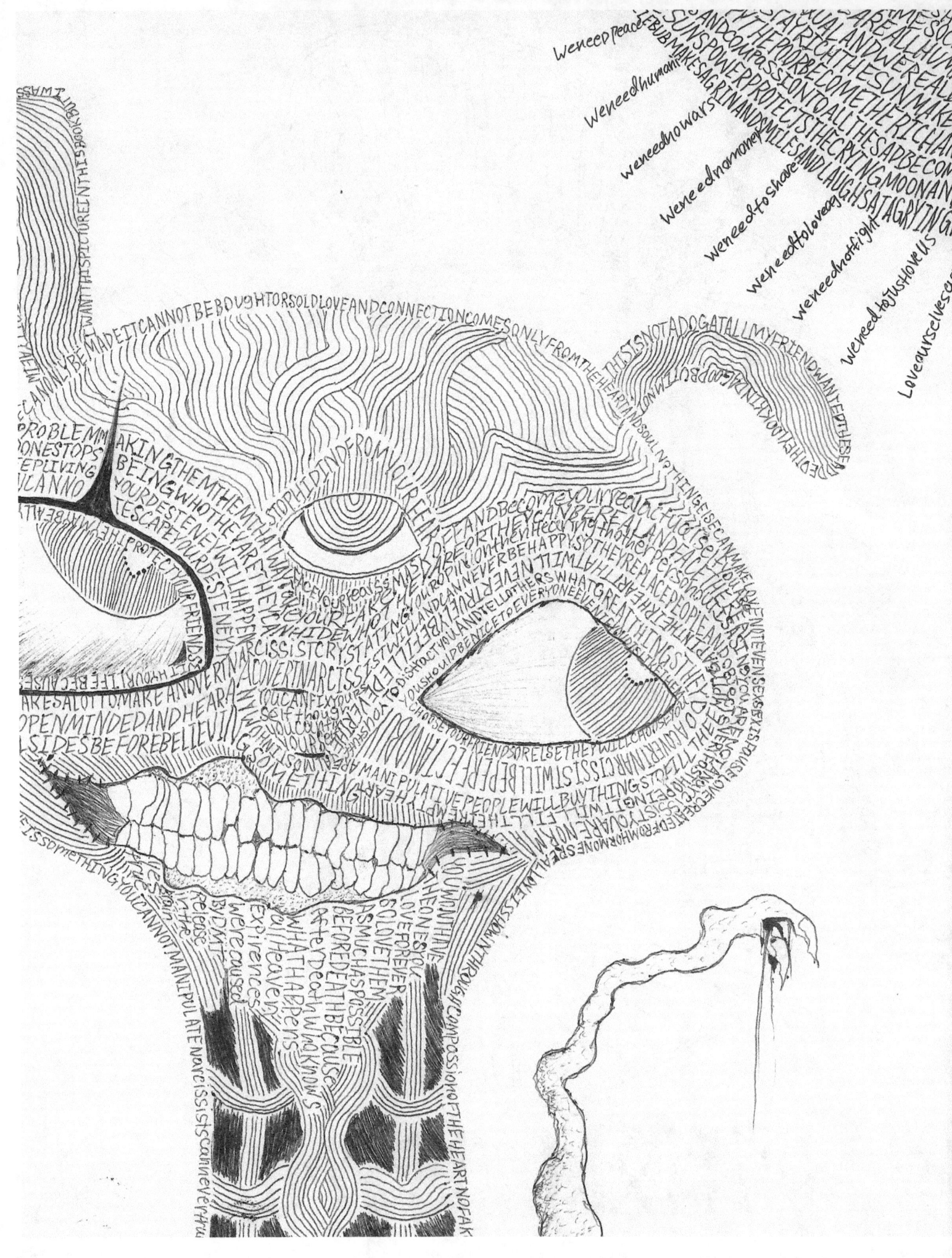

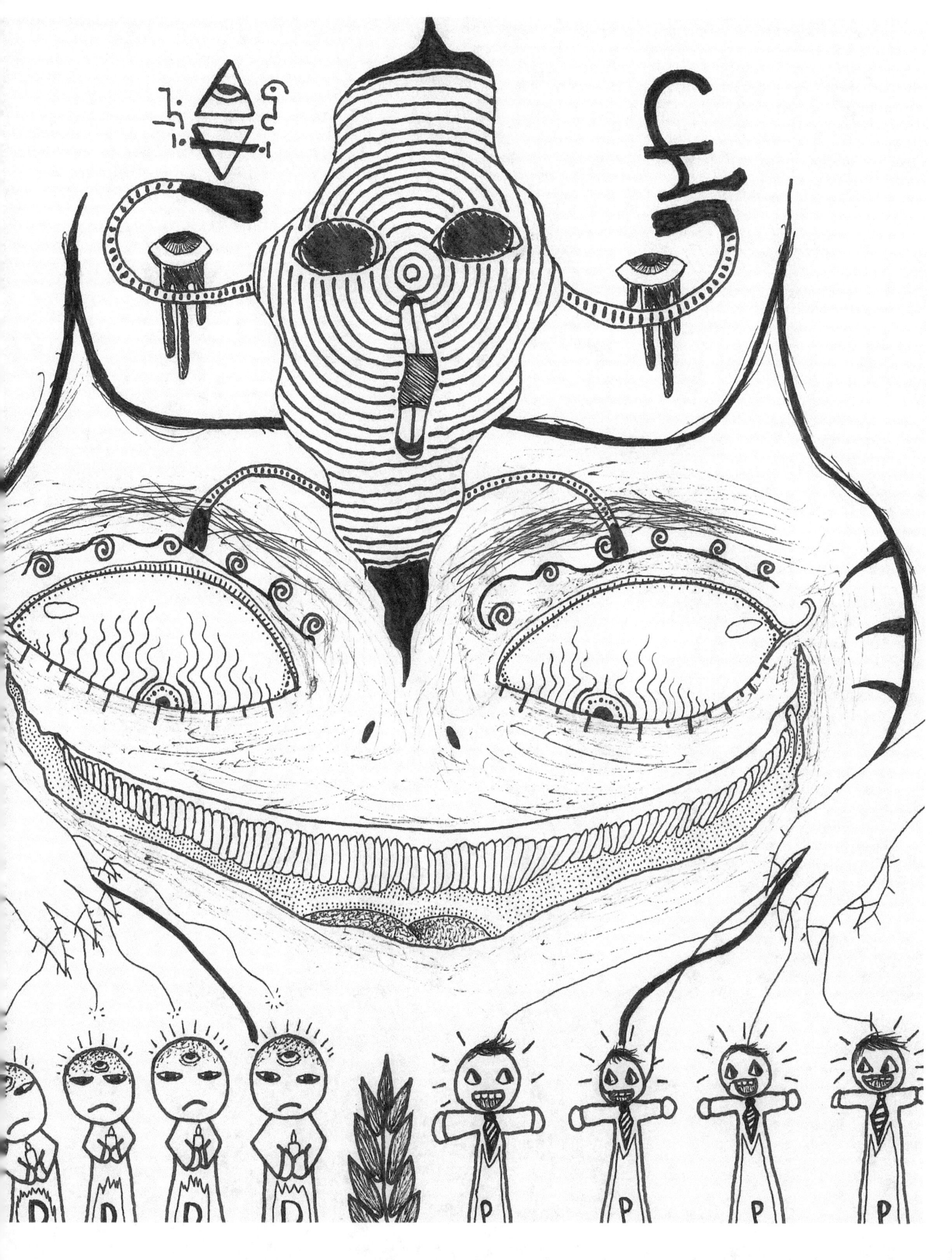

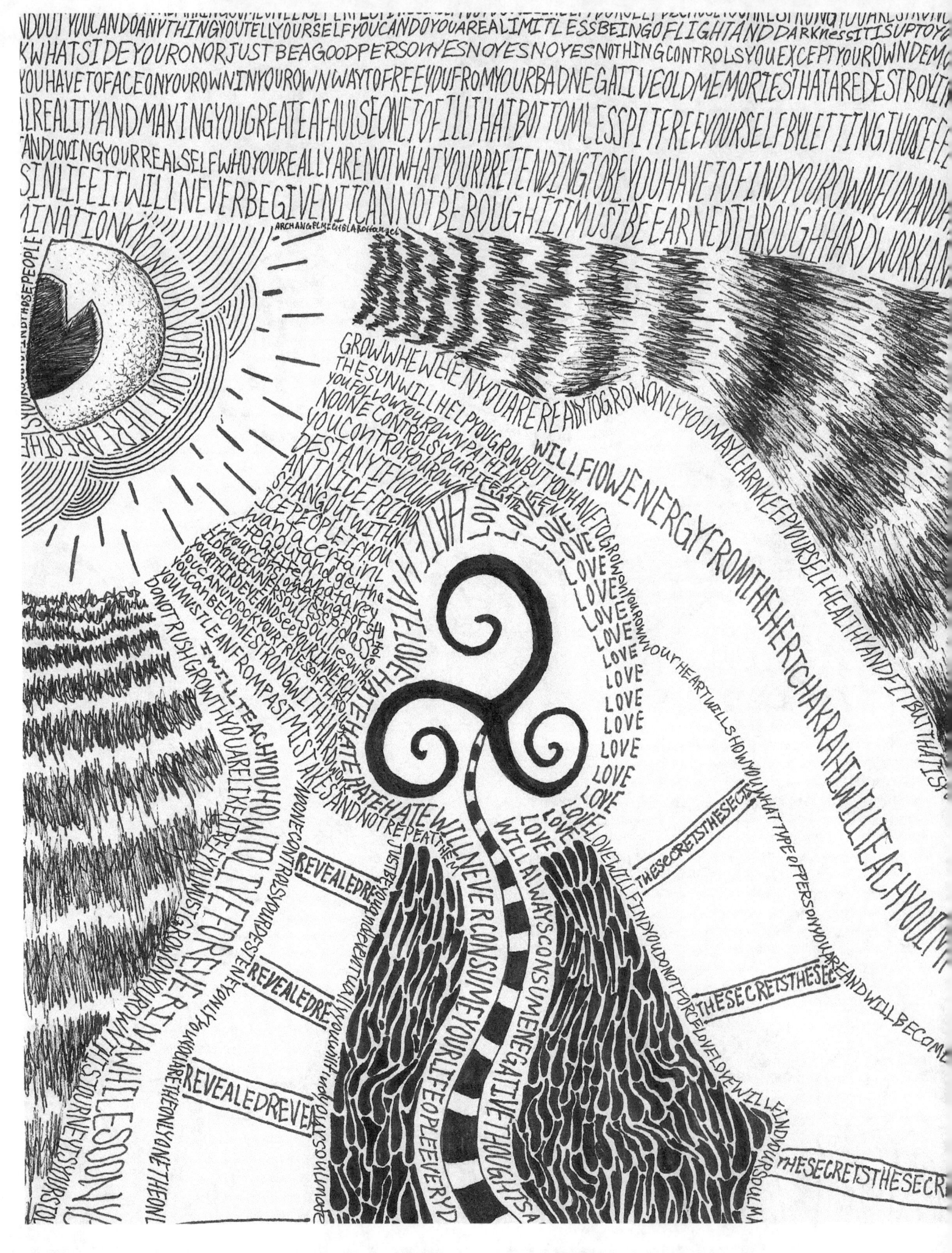

LOVE

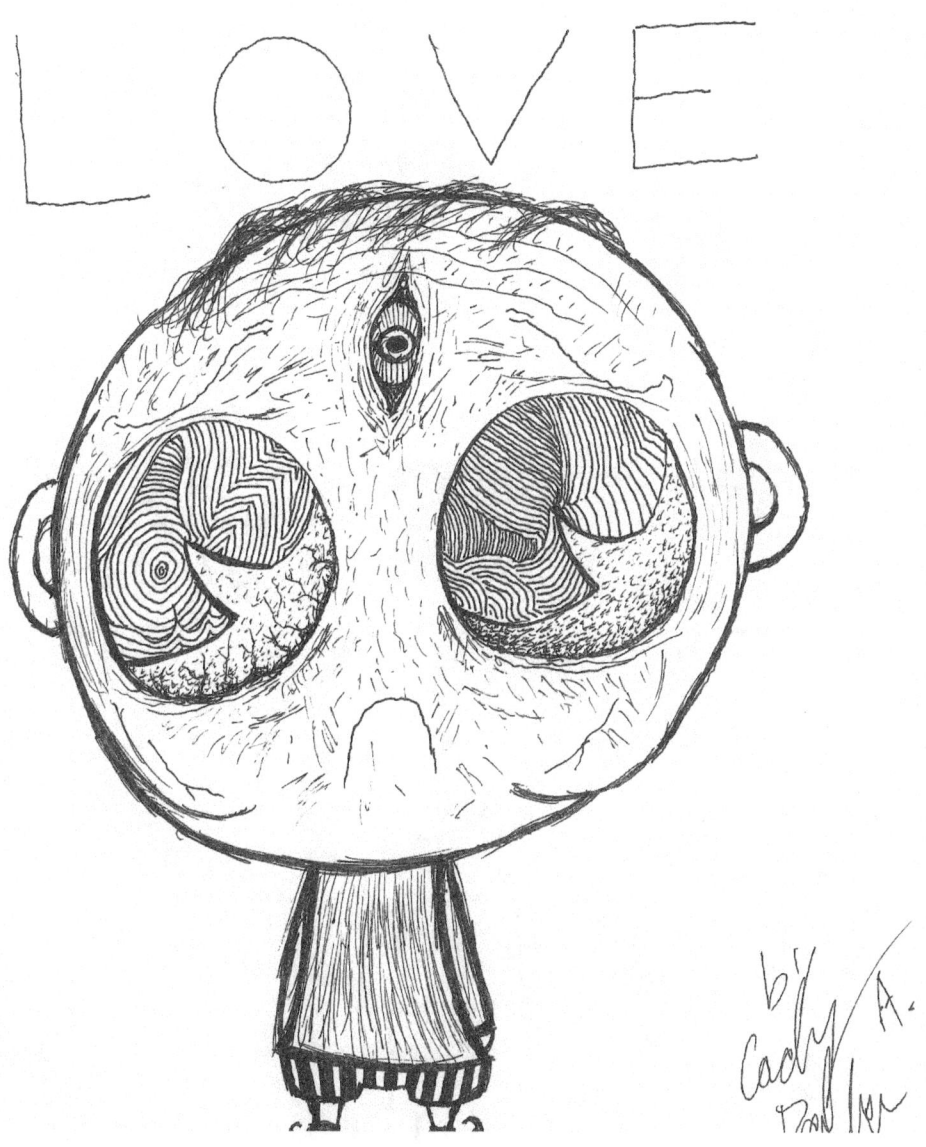

by Cady A.
[signature]

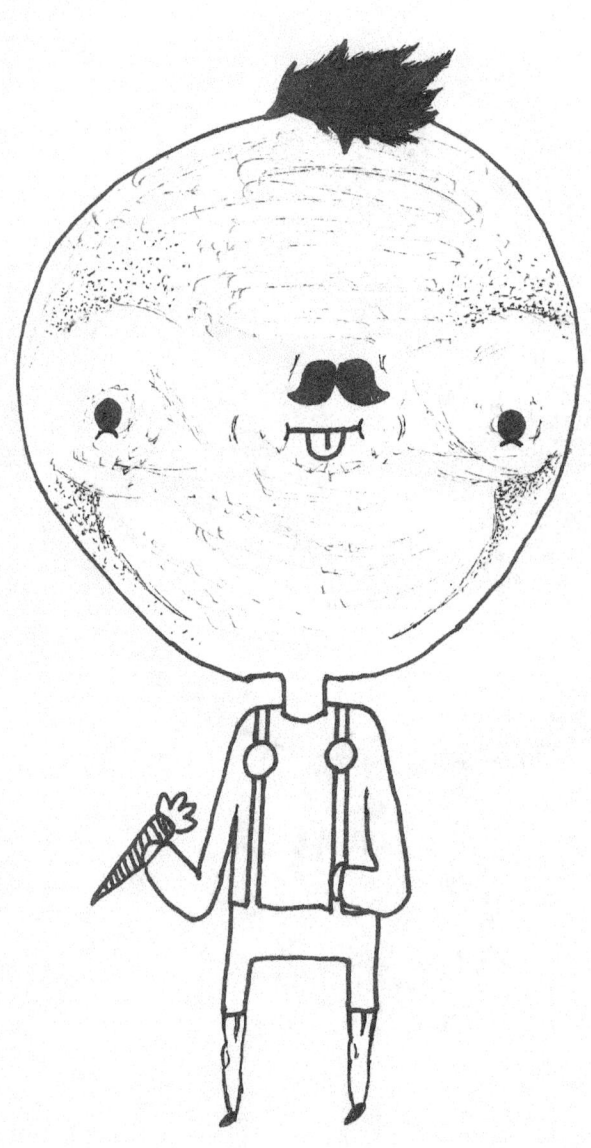

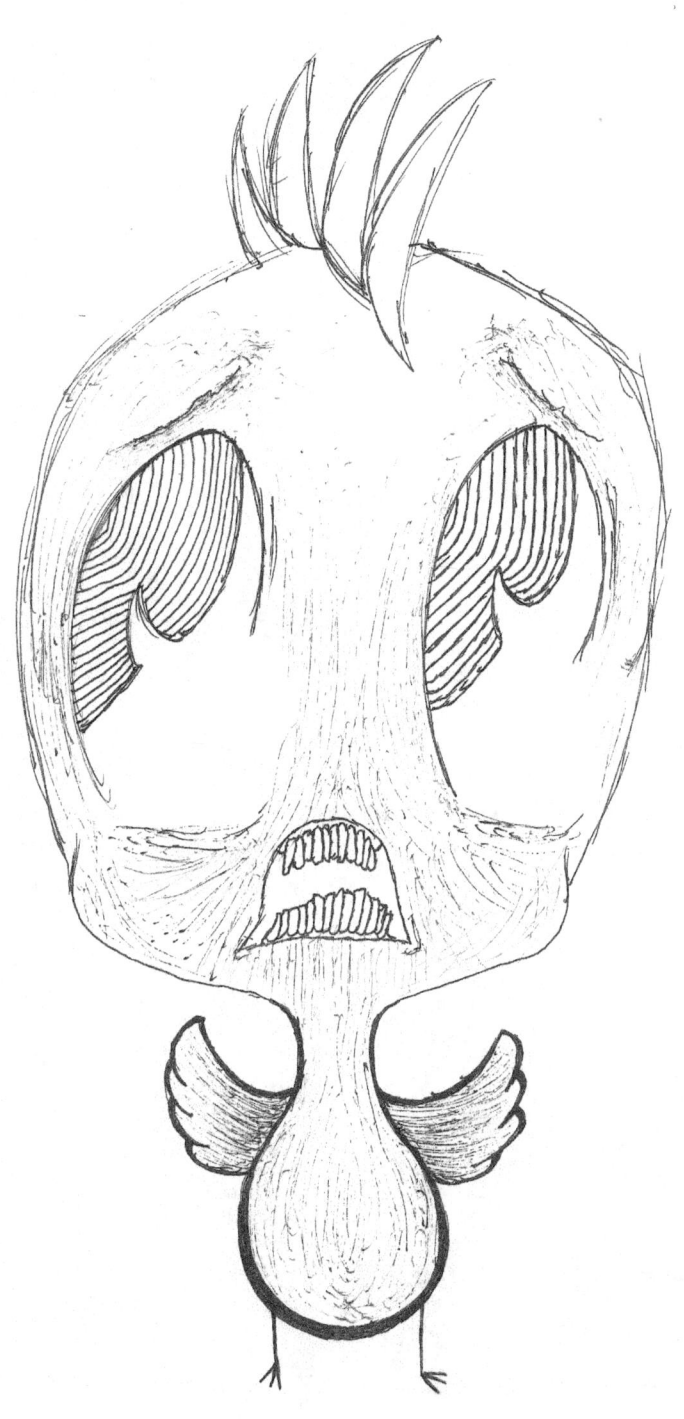

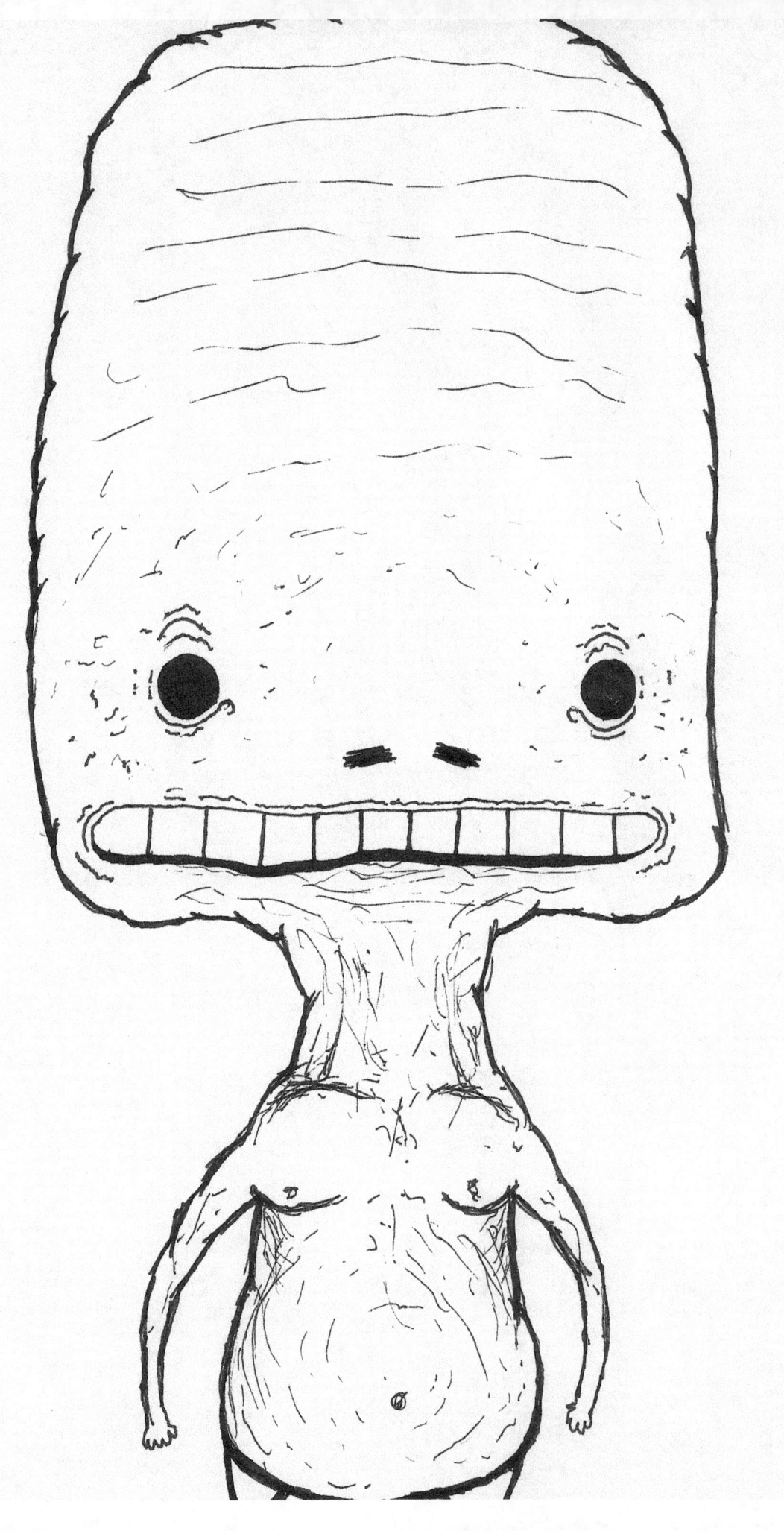

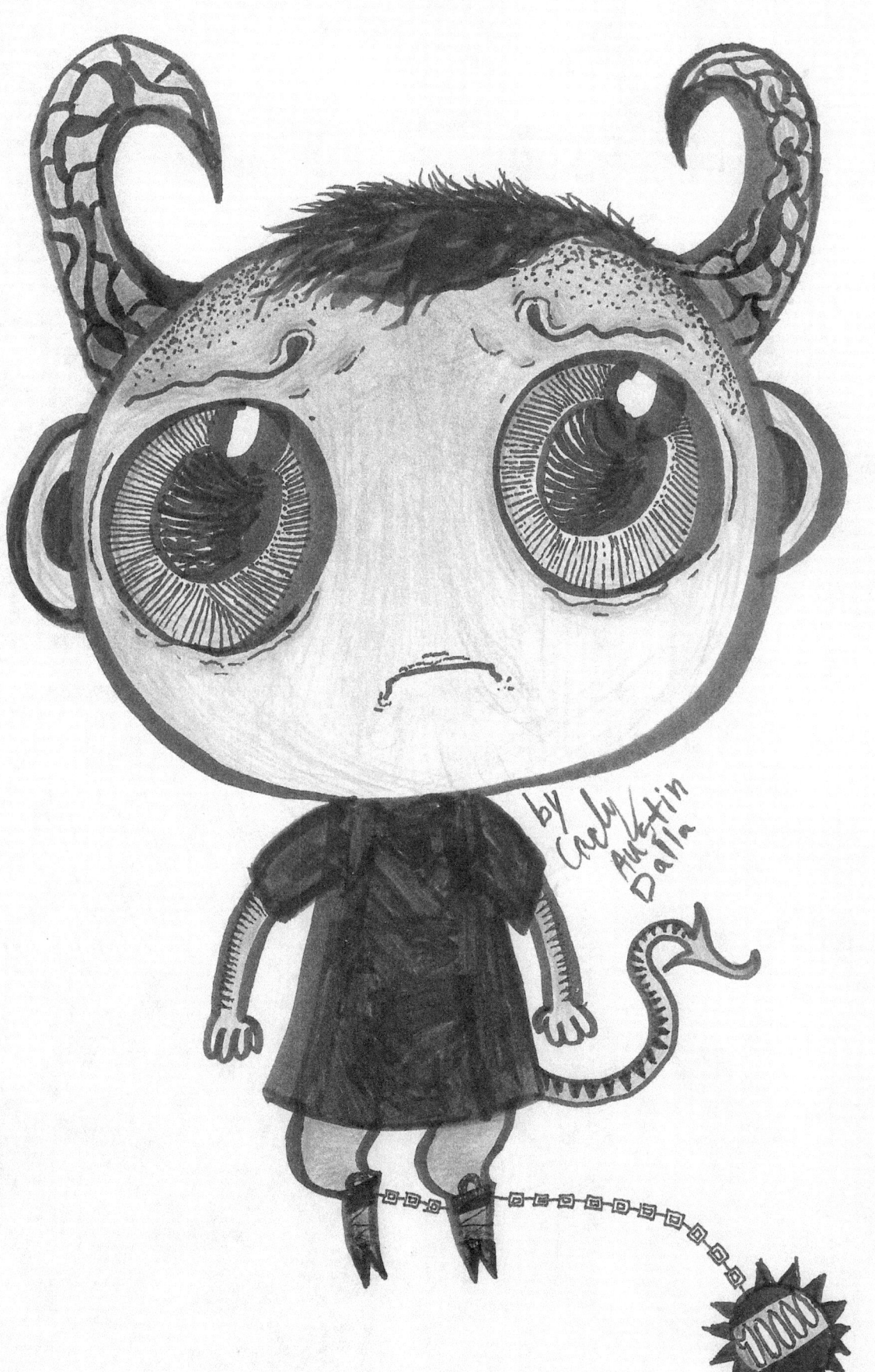
by Caely
Austin
Dalla

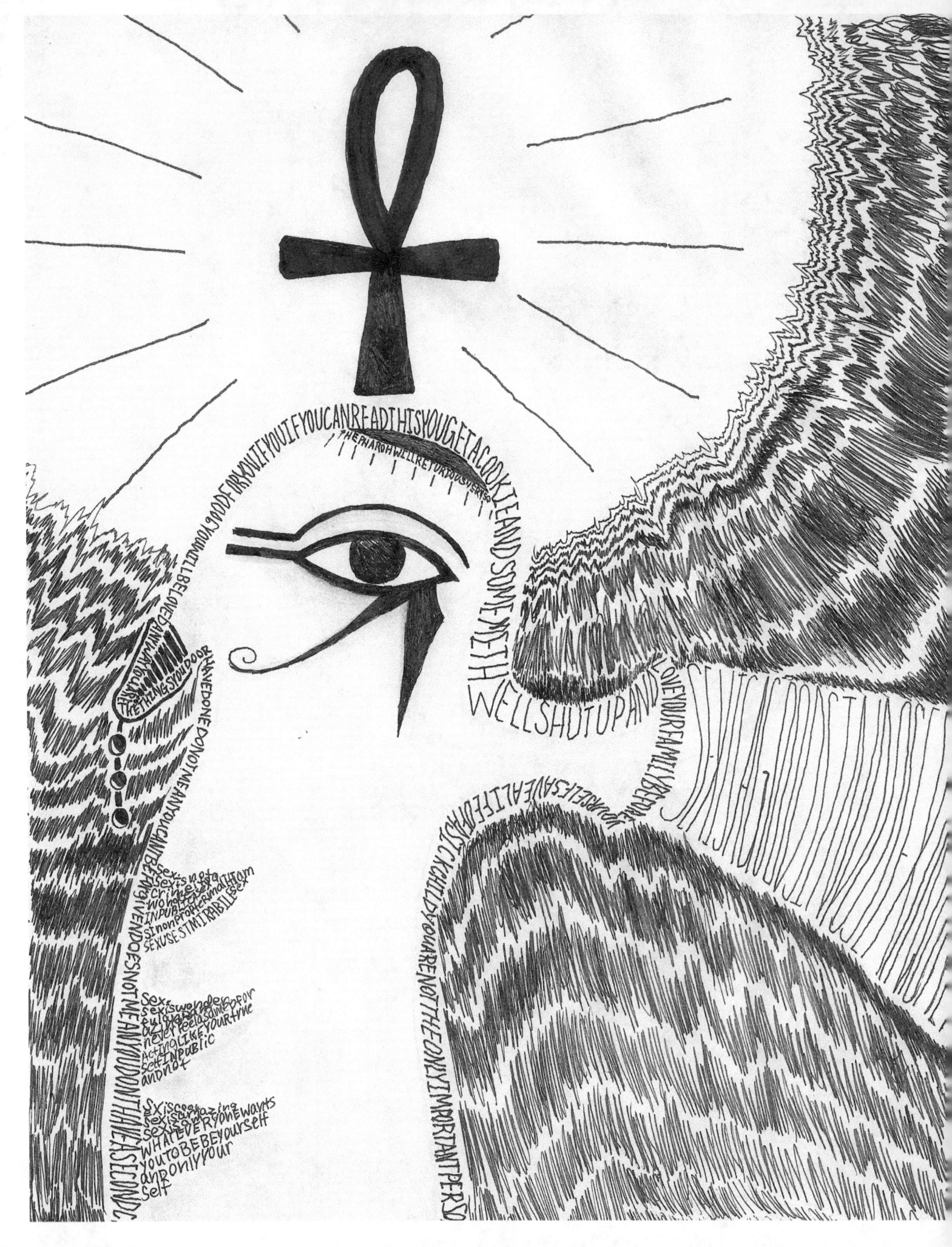

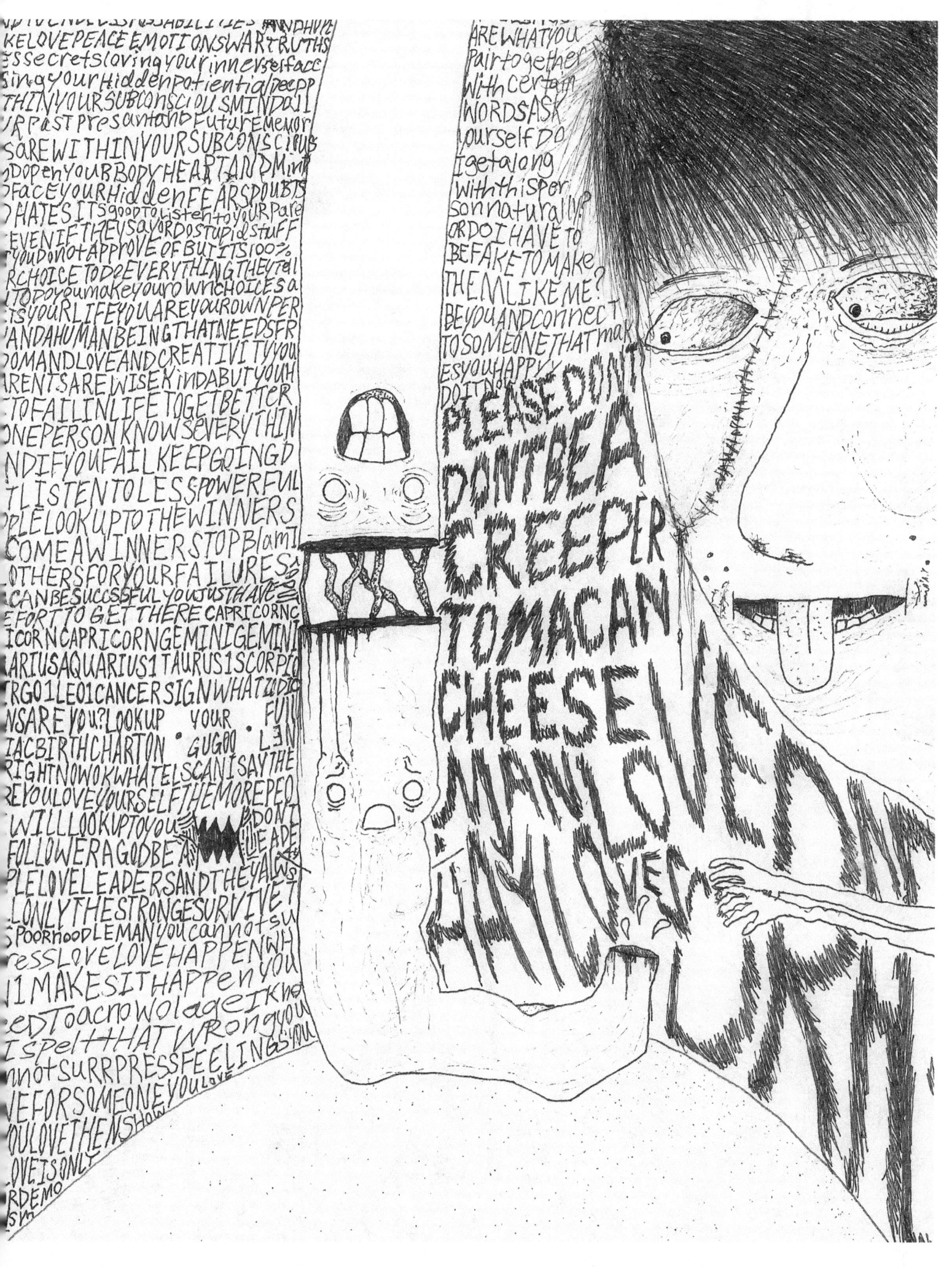

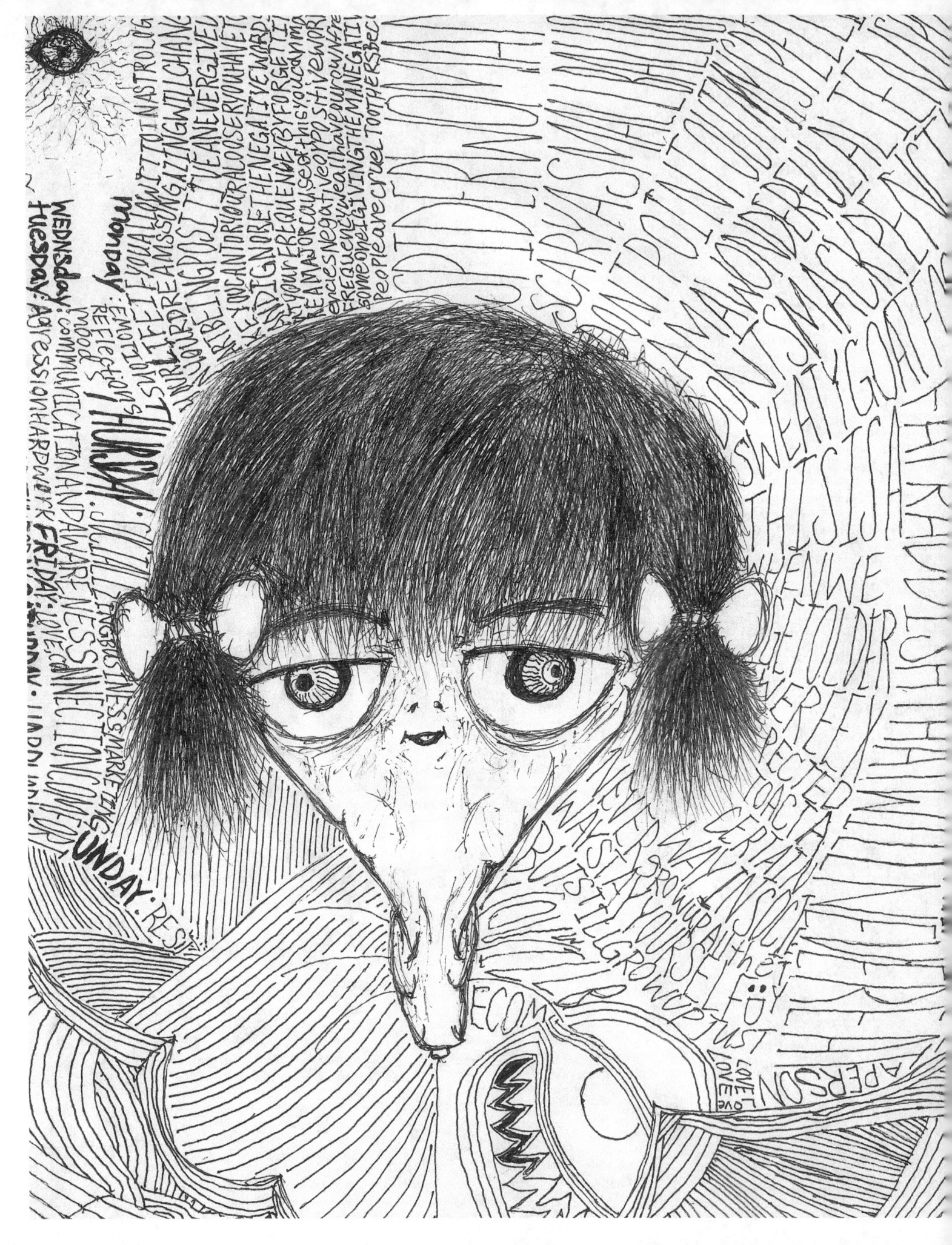

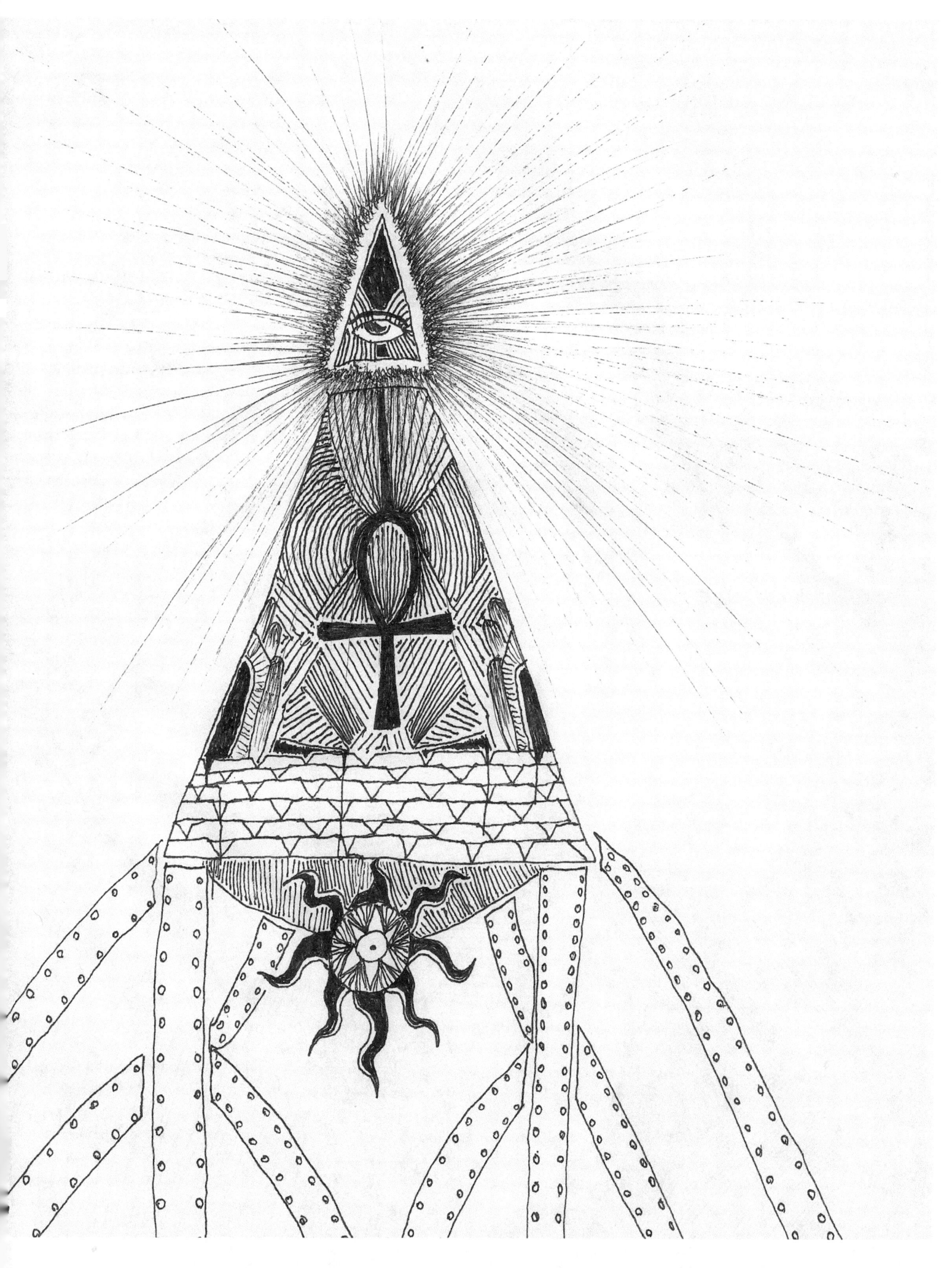

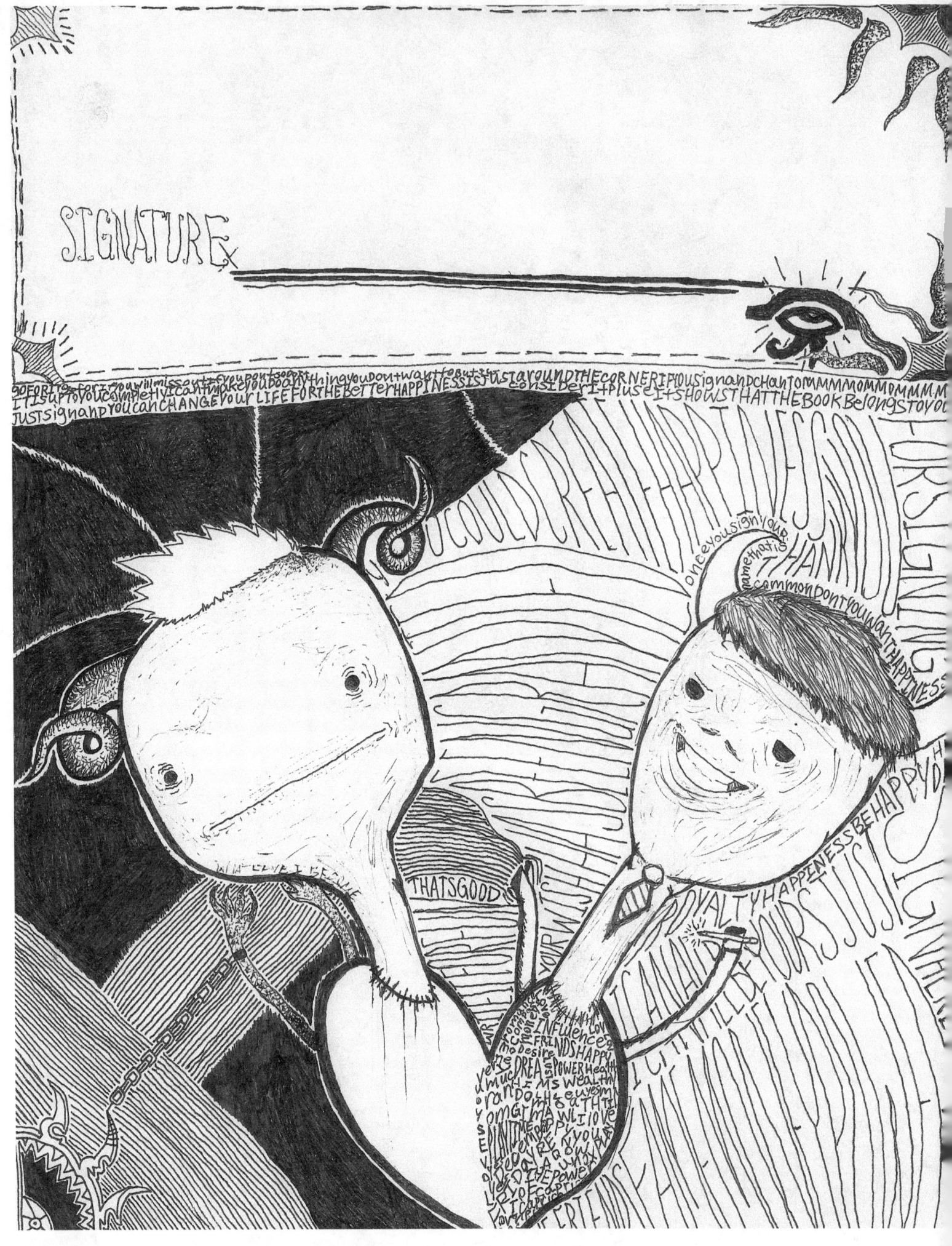